# Everything

## Words and Music by
## Amy Foster-Gillies,
## Michael Bublé and Alan Chang

## Arranged for harp by Sylvia Woods

# Everything

**Lever harp players**: set your sharping levers for the key signature, and then re-set the levers shown above.

**Pedal harp players**: you may play E-flats whenever there are D-sharps if you prefer.  Change the pedal markings accordingly.

Sharping lever changes are indicated with diamond notes and also with octave wording.
Pedal changes are written below the bass staff.

Words and Music by Amy Foster-Gillies,
Michael Bublé and Alan Chang

Harp arrangement by Sylvia Woods

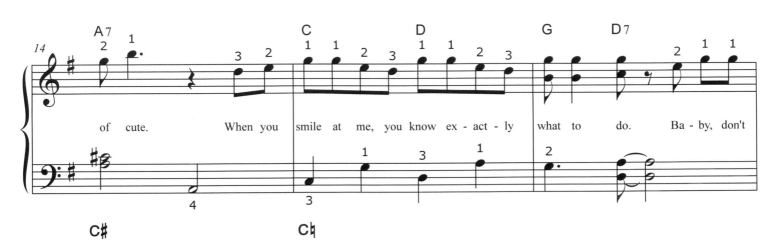

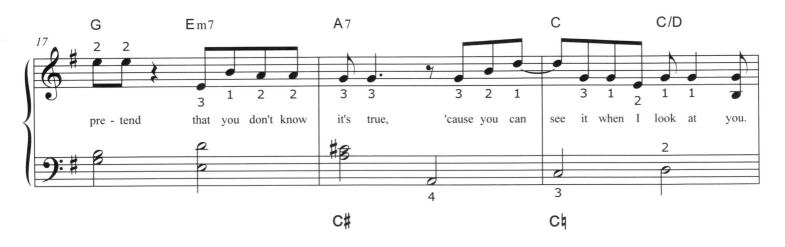

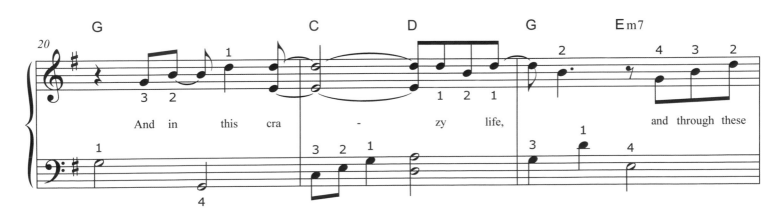

Everything

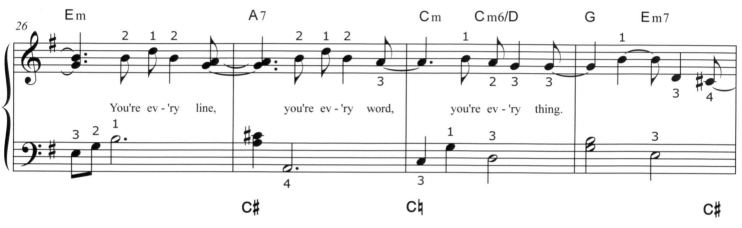

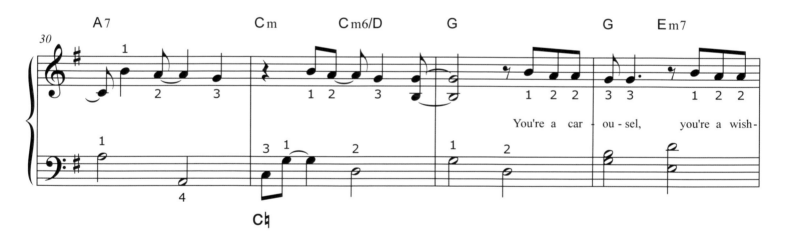

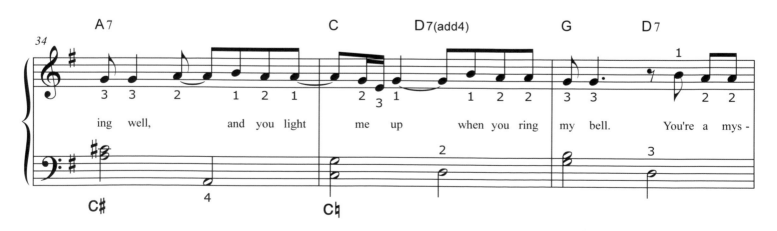

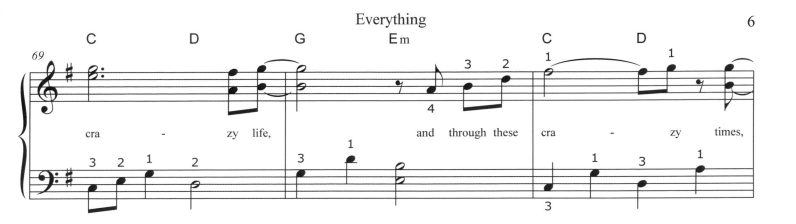

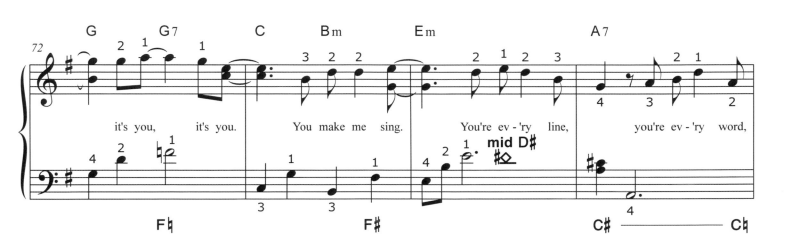

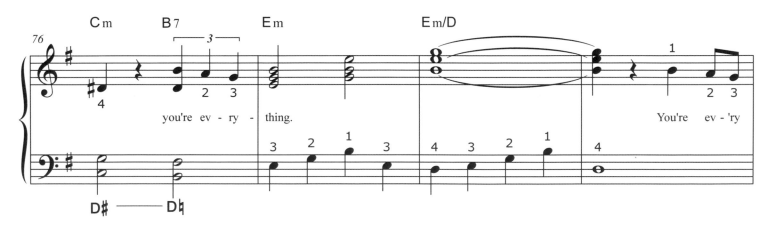

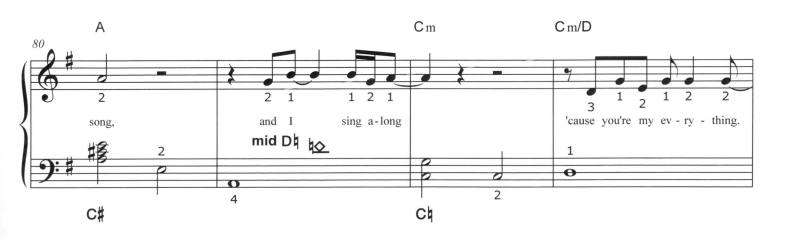

Everything

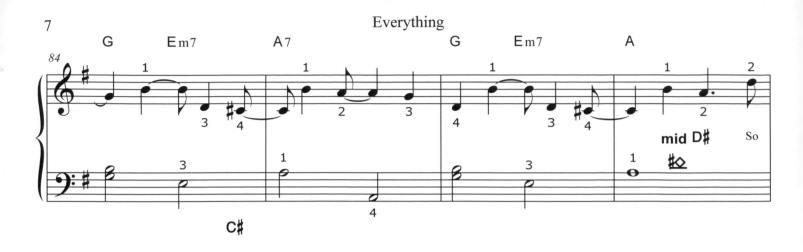

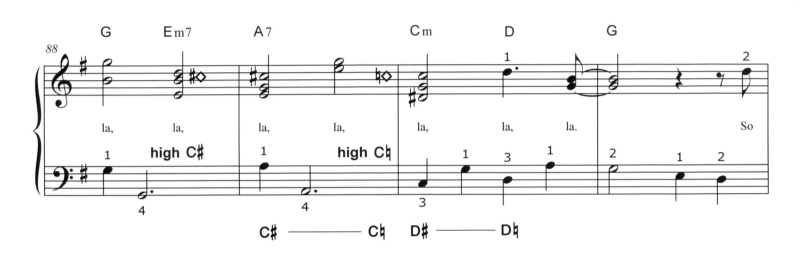

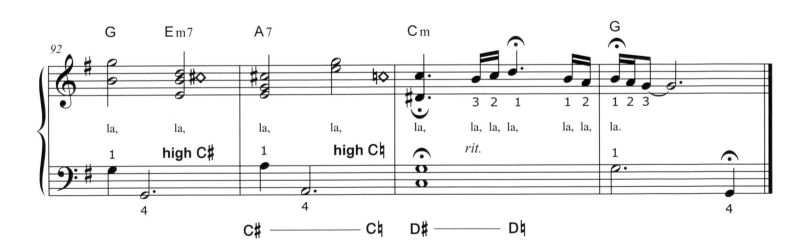